JUL   2013

D1205532

SMART ABOUT SPORTS

Meet the Colts

By

Mike Kennedy

with Mark Stewart

NORWOOD HOUSE PRESS

Norwood House Press, P.O. Box 316598, Chicago, Illinois 60631

For information regarding Norwood House Press,
please visit our website at: www.norwoodhousepress.com or call 866-565-2900.

Photo Credits:
   Getty Images (4, 7, 8, 12, 13, 15, 16, 18, 20, 21, 22), Black Book Partners (23).
Cover Photos:
   Top Left: Topps, Inc.; Top Right: Bob Levey/Icon SMI; Bottom Left: Icon SMI; Bottom Right: Topps, Inc.
The football memorabilia photographed for this book is part of the authors' collection:
   Page 6) Jim Parker: Philadelphia Gum Company, Page 10) Gino Marchetti: TCMA, Ltd.;
   Raymond Berry, Bert Jones & Johnny Unitas: Topps, Inc., Page 11) Marvin Harrison,
   Dwight Freeney & Peyton Manning: Topps, Inc.; Edgerrin James: The Upper Deck Company.
Special thanks to Topps, Inc.

Editor: Brian Fitzgerald
Designer: Ron Jaffe
Project Management: Black Book Partners, LLC.
Editorial Production: Jessica McCulloch

LIBRARY OF CONGRESS CATALOGING-IN-PUBLICATION DATA
   Kennedy, Mike.
      Meet the Colts / By Mike Kennedy with Mark Stewart.
         p. cm. -- (Smart about sports)
      Includes bibliographical references and index.
      Summary: "An introductory look at the Indianapolis Colts football team.
   Includes a brief history, facts, photos, records, glossary, and fun
   activities"--Provided by publisher.
      ISBN-13: 978-1-59953-394-0 (library edition : alk. paper)
      ISBN-10: 1-59953-394-4 (library edition : alk. paper)
      1. Indianapolis Colts (Football team)--History--Juvenile literature. I.
   Stewart, Mark. II. Title.
      GV956.I53K46 2010
      796.332'640977252--dc22
                                    2010008304

Manufactured in the United States of America in North Mankato, Minnesota.
179R—042011

Contents

Words in **bold type** are defined on page 24.

Victory! Coach Tony Dungy and Peyton Manning are champions.

The Indianapolis Colts

A winning team starts with a good quarterback. The Indianapolis Colts know this is true. They have had some of the best in the National Football League (NFL).

Once Upon a Time

The Colts played their first season in Indianapolis in 1984. Before that, they played in Baltimore, Maryland. They 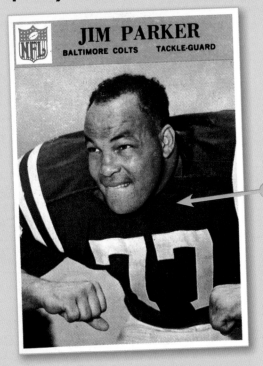 have won titles in both cities. They have put many great players on the field. Jim Parker and Bubba Smith were two of the best.

Bubba Smith was a leader of the team's defense.

The stadium roof is open for a game.

At the Stadium

The team's home field is Lucas Oil Stadium. If the weather is good, the roof can be opened. If not, the roof stays closed. Fans watch replays on two big screens. They can also see the city through a wall of windows.

Shoe Box

The cards on these pages belong to the authors. They show some of the best Colts ever.

Gino Marchetti

Defensive Lineman
- 1953–1964 & 1966

Gino Marchetti loved to tackle quarterbacks. His best moves are still used today.

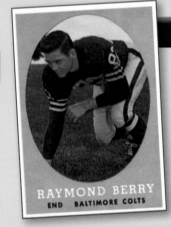

RAYMOND BERRY
END   BALTIMORE COLTS

Raymond Berry

Receiver
- 1955–1967

Raymond Berry almost never dropped a pass.

Johnny Unitas

Quarterback
- 1956–1972

Johnny Unitas never gave up on any game.

JOHNNY
UNITAS
COLTS
QUARTERBACK

Bert Jones

Quarterback
- 1973–1981

Bert Jones had a great arm. He threw lots of long passes.

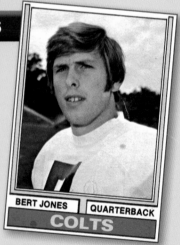

BERT JONES | QUARTERBACK
COLTS

Marvin Harrison

Receiver • 1996–2008
Marvin Harrison scored 128 **touchdowns** for the team.

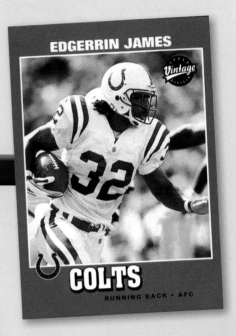

Edgerrin James

Running Back • 1999–2005
Edgerrin James could run with the ball and also catch passes.

Peyton Manning

Quarterback • 1998–
Peyton Manning always knew what the defense was going to do. His father was a star quarterback, too.

Dwight Freeney

Defensive Lineman • 2002–
Dwight Freeney used speed and power to make tackles.

11

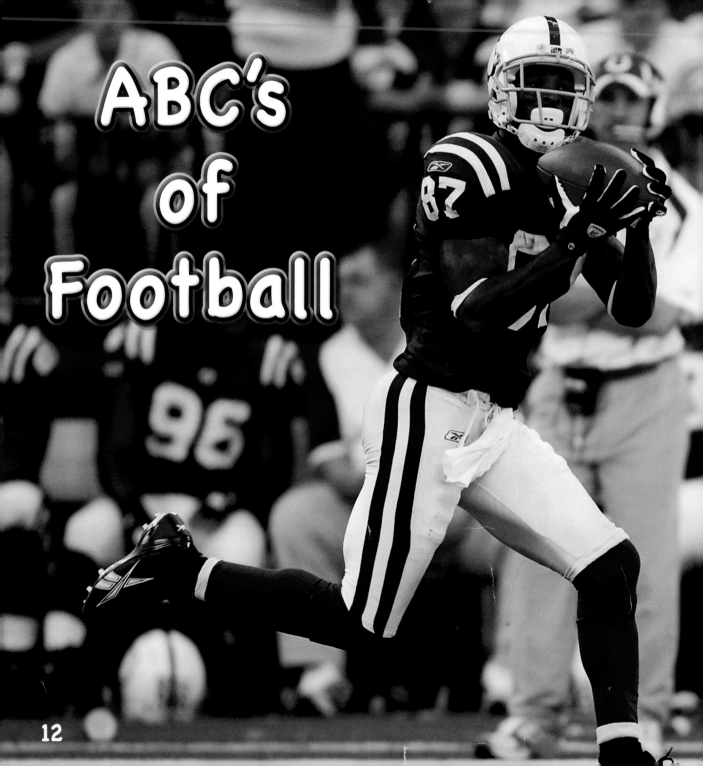

ABC's
of
Football

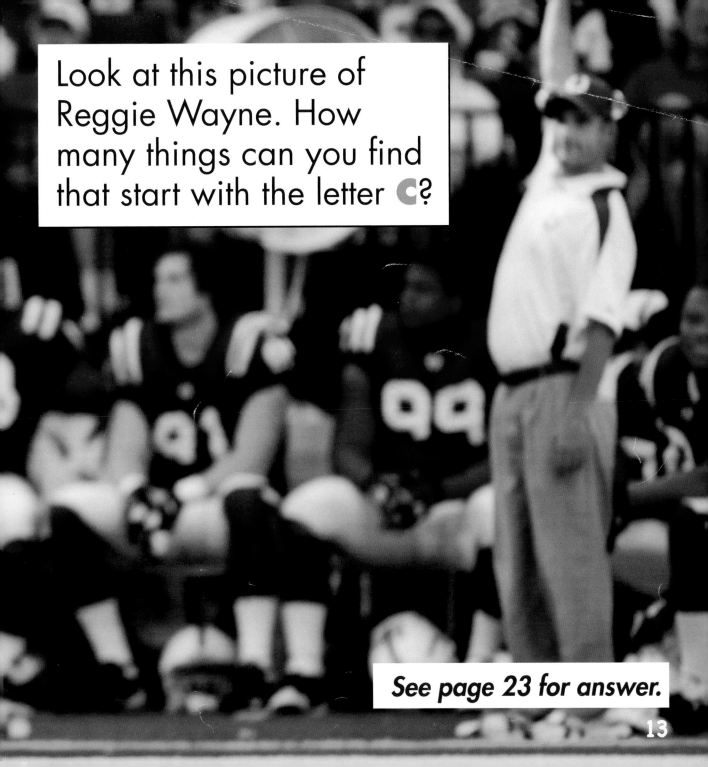

Look at this picture of Reggie Wayne. How many things can you find that start with the letter C?

See page 23 for answer.

Brain Games

Here is a poem about a famous Colt:

There once was a speedster named Lenny.
His highlights and touchdowns were many.
Uniform wearers
Hoped he'd make errors.
But they found he didn't make any.

Guess which one of these facts is **TRUE**:

- *Lenny Moore led the NFL in touchdowns in 1964.*

- *Lenny never played in the **Pro Bowl**.*

See page 23 for answer.

Johnny Unitas hands the ball to Lenny Moore.

Blue pumps up the fans before a game.

Fun on the Field

The Colts and their fans are like a big family. Blue adds to the team spirit. He is the team mascot. He has fun with the fans before, during, and after games.

On the Map

The Colts call Indianapolis, Indiana home.
The players come from all over the world.
These Colts played in the Pro Bowl. Match
each with the place he was born:

1 **Art Donovan • Pro Bowl: 1953–1957**
Bronx, New York

2 **Alan Ameche • Pro Bowl: 1955–1958**
Kenosha, Wisconsin

3 **Ted Hendricks • Pro Bowl: 1971–1973**
Guatemala City, Guatemala

4 **Eric Dickerson**
• Pro Bowl: 1987–1989
Sealy, Texas

5 **Marshall Faulk**
• Pro Bowl: 1994,
1995 & 1998
New Orleans, Louisiana

The Colts play
in Indianapolis, Indiana.

World Map

What's in the Locker?

The team's home uniform has a blue shirt with white stripes. The pants are white with blue stripes.

Robert Mathis wears the team's home uniform.

The team's road uniform has a white shirt with blue stripes. The team always wears a white helmet. It has a blue horseshoe on each side.

Dallas Clark wears the team's road uniform.

We Won!

The Colts won their first NFL title in 1958.

They scored the winning touchdown on the game's last play. The Colts won **Super Bowl** 41 for their fifth title.

It's good! Jim O'Brien jumps high after making the winning kick in Super Bowl 5.

Record Book

These Colts stars set team records.

Running Back	Record	Year
Lenny Moore	20 total touchdowns	1964
Eric Dickerson	388 carries	1988
Edgerrin James	1,709 **yards**	2000

Quarterback/Receiver	Record	Year
Roger Carr	25.9 yards per catch	1976
Marvin Harrison	143 catches	2002
Peyton Manning	49 touchdown passes	2004

Answer for ABC's of Football

Here are some words in the picture that start with C:
Chin Strap, Cleats, Colts Uniform.
Did you find any others?

Answer for Brain Games

The first fact is true. Lenny Moore scored 20 touchdowns in 1964. He played in the Pro Bowl seven times.

Football Words

PRO BOWL
A special game played between the NFL's top stars.

SUPER BOWL
The game that decides the champion of the NFL.

TOUCHDOWNS
Scoring plays worth six points.

YARDS
A yard is a distance of three feet. A football field is 100 yards from goal line to goal line.

Index

Photos are on **bold** numbered pages.

About the Colts

Learn more about the Colts at www.colts.com

Learn more about football at www.profootballhof.com